COMPLETE PRIMARY ENGLISH LANGUAGE PROG

Luna's Es

Mary O'Keeffe

GILL EDUCATION

It was **spring**.

Everyone was in the garden.

We all had our **wellies** on.

I was busy helping Auntie Emma.

Meg and Mel were jumping in the dirt in their **wellies**!

Luna was in the garden, looking here and looking there.

Luna liked to dig in the turf too!

We did a lot of work.

"Tom, will you go in and get us four nut bars?" said Auntie Emma. "Quick, before Meg and Mel go for the worms!"

Luna! Luna!

Mam had Luna's **lead**.

"Luna!" said Mam. "Come and let me put on your **lead**! Does anyone want to come to the park? Luna?"

"Oh no!" cried Auntie Emma. "There's a big gap in the old **fence**. Luna is not here."

"It will be okay," said Mam. "She won't go too far."

Thank you, Mr Ford!

Not long after, there was a buzz at the front door.

Mr Ford was there.

He had a firm hand on Luna's collar.

"She wanted to play with my Marvin," he said.

Meg and Mel made a big fuss, petting Luna's fur.

Luna gave my arm a big lick.

"Okay, Luna," said Dad, "no more escapes! Let's fix the **fence**."

We set off for the **garden centre**.

Auntie Emma, Meg, Mel and Luna went to the park.

There would be no room for them in the car.

On the way in, Dad got a big cart.

First, we had to get a new bit of **fence**.

"How many parts do we need, Dad?" I asked.

"I'd say four," he said.

Next, Dad got a hammer, a ruler and some cord.

Mam picked up a little **saw** and some sandpaper.

"What's that for?" I asked.

Mam gave me a wink and said, "You'll see!"

"Can we put some colour on the **fence**?" I asked.

"You must like hard work!" said Beth. "I can help you. Come over here."

Basil, mint, dill and bay… These will all be yummy in lots of dinners.

Lastly, Mam got some herbs for the garden.

"I will help you to water them," I said.

We went to the till to pay.

Mam and Dad packed up the car and off we went.

When we got back, we all got to work.

Auntie Emma put the herbs in the border next to the back door.

Meg and Mel helped her to dig.

Poor Luna!

I went in and gave her a pet.

When I got back, Mam had used the **saw** to cut a circle in the **fence**.

"What is that circle for, Mam?" I asked.

"Well," said Mam, "Luna goes missing so that she can visit her pal Marvin. Now they can see each other, so there will be no need for Luna to escape again."

Super idea, Mam!